Guidance and
Behavior Management

Join us on the Web at

EarlyChildEd.delmar.com

Guidance and Behavior Management

Teresa Frazier

THOMSON

™

DELMAR LEARNING

Australia • Canada • Mexico • Singapore • Spain • United Kingdom • United States

ISBN-13: 978-1-4180-3098-8
ISBN-10: 1-4180-3098-8

Library of Congress Catalog Card Number:2006008007

NOTICE TO THE READER
The authors and Thomson Delmar Learning affirm that the Web site URLs referenced herein were accurate at the time of printing. However, due to the fluid nature of the Internet, we cannot guarantee their accuracy for the life of the edition.

TABLE OF CONTENTS

INTRODUCTION

Throughout a college preparation program to become an early childhood educator, students take many courses and read many textbooks. Their knowledge grows as they accumulate ideas from lectures, reading, experiences, and discussions. When they finish their coursework, graduate, and move into their first teaching positions, students often leave behind some of the books they have used. The hope is, however, that they take with them the important ideas from their classes and books as they begin their own professional practice.

More experienced colleagues or mentors sometimes support teachers in their first teaching positions, helping them make the transition from the college classroom to being responsible for a group of young children. Other times, new teachers are left to travel their own paths, relying on their own resources. Whatever your situation, this professional enhancement guide is designed to provide reminders of what you have learned, as well as resources to help you make sense of and apply that knowledge.

Teachers of young children are under great pressure today. Families demand support in their difficult tasks of child-rearing in today's fast-paced and changing world. Some families become so overwhelmed with the tasks of parenting that they seem to leave too much responsibility on the shoulders of teachers and caregivers. From administrators and institutions, there are expectations that sometimes seem overwhelming. Teachers are being held accountable for children's learning in ways unprecedented in even the recent past. Public scrutiny has led to insistence on teaching practices that may seem contrary to the best interests of children or their teachers. New teachers may find themselves caught between the realities of the schools or centers where they are working, and their own philosophies and ideals of working with children. When faced with such dilemmas, these individuals need to be able to fall back and reflect on what they know of best practices, renewing their professional determination to make appropriate decisions for children.

This book provides similar tools for that reflection:

- Tips for getting off to a great start in your new environment

- Information about typical developmental patterns of children from birth through school age

- Suggestions for materials that promote development for children from infancy through the primary grades

- Tools to assist teachers in observing children and gathering data to help set appropriate goals for individual children

- Guides for planning appropriate classroom experiences and sample lesson plans

- Tips for introducing children to the joys of literacy

- A summary of the key ideas about developmentally appropriate practice, the process of decision making that allows teachers to provide optimum environments for children from birth through school age

- Professional development resources for teachers

- Ideas for locating lists of other resources

- Case studies of relevant, realistic situations you may face, as well as best practices for successfully navigating them

- Insight into issues and trends facing early childhood educators today

- Enlarged margins for notes

Becoming a teacher is a continuing process of growing, learning, reflecting, and discovering through experience. Having these resources will help you along your way. Good luck on your journey!

PREFACE

Our world has changed dramatically in the past few years. Behavioral management techniques that may have worked a few years ago have no impact on children today. Have children changed or have adults changed?

Technology has quickened the pace of life today. We are expected to "stay in touch" all the time—whether it is work, school, or recreation. Parents are frazzled trying to provide their children with opportunities to be successful adults—even if that means taking away their childhood. Adults know how hard it is to find a good job today and that their children need much more than just an education to "get ahead." So we cart our children to soccer practice, violin, piano, gymnastics, dance, skating, tee ball, hockey, and horseback riding. Children are given hours worth of homework each night as well. Rarely do families sit down each night to dinner. More often, dinner is a quick stop at the local fast-food restaurant.

Parents blame teachers and teachers blame parents for the children's behavioral problems. It is hard to believe that parents don't care enough about their children to teach them right from wrong. So why are children kicked out of preschool or child care? What would cause a four-year-old to say he wishes he was dead? Middle school students try to poison their teachers, and teenagers kill classmates and parents. What could have been done to prevent such tragedies? How can we stop this from happening again? The answer is YOU. You can make a difference in a child's life—one step at a time.

The purpose of this book is to help you, the new teacher, develop the necessary skills to encourage healthy emotional development and to ensure that children will become caring, well-adjusted individuals.

This tool was developed to help you, the budding teacher and/or child care provider, as you move into your first classroom. The editors at Thomson Delmar Learning encourage and appreciate your feedback on this or any of our other products.

Go to http://www.earlychilded.delmar.com and click on the "Professional Enhancement series feedback" link to let us know what you think.

1

BEHAVIOR MANAGEMENT BASICS

INTRODUCTION

Discipline, behavior management, guidance, punishment—we hear these words every day. What do they mean? Does it matter what terminology we use with children? With parents? Why should we even know what these words mean? "The only thing that matters is that the children do what I tell them, when I tell them! It doesn't matter how or what I say to them." Right? Wrong!

Parents want their children to grow up and become productive adults who are responsible and well adjusted. This does not just happen. Infants are born not knowing right from wrong. Our job is to nurture and guide them during the first few years of their lives. Doing this requires parents and teachers working together as a team.

DISCIPLINE

Discipline is defined as "a system of rules governing conduct," "training that corrects, molds, or perfects" (Lingren, 1996), or "to teach and to train." In contrast, **punishment** refers to punitive suffering, pain, and loss. The purpose of discipline then is to help children learn self-control and grow into responsible adults. Punishment focuses on bad behavior instead of encouraging good behavior.

Ineffective discipline teaches children to obey when an adult is watching, be concerned only for themselves, view parents and teachers as a threat, and think they can do what they want as long as they don't get "caught." Ineffective discipline also teaches that threatening and hurting people allows them to "get what they want." Effective discipline helps a child develop self-discipline, responsibility, and positive self-esteem and teaches a child to respect parents, teachers, and others.

How can a teacher help a child achieve these goals? First, the teacher needs to evaluate himself or herself. Everyone needs to feel important—children and adults alike. For a teacher to help children feel good about themselves, the teacher must first feel good about himself or herself. We must take care of our own physical and emotional well-being. Children as well as adults need to have their most basic needs met. Maslow's Hierarchy of Needs explains what those needs are (Figure 1-1).

Maslow

Maslow proposed that certain needs must be met to develop a healthy personality. Those basic needs are physiological needs, safety needs, belonging and love needs, and self-esteem needs. If these needs are met, Maslow believed a person would ultimately become a fully functional individual. This theory is often referred

Figure 1-1 Maslow's Hierarchy of Needs

to as the hierarchy of needs and is shown as a pyramid with physiological needs serving as the basis for higher growth needs (refer to Figure 1-1). Examples of physiological needs include food, water, sleep, and warmth. We need a roof over our heads to provide these basic necessities. Safety needs include feeling a sense of psychological security and freedom from fear. We must feel secure from danger. Needs of belonging and love are met when a person is provided with affection and acceptance by those who care for him or her on a consistent basis. We need to feel loved. Esteem needs follow with a child feeling competent and experiencing approval and recognition for his or her accomplishments. We need to feel valued. Higher growth needs relate to an individual's developing knowledge and understanding in defining the meaning of concepts such as goodness, order, and justice. All these levels lead to the process of self-actualization.

A child may have his physiological, safety, security, and love and belonging needs met only to become homeless when a parent loses a job. The fear of being hungry and having no place to sleep will cause the child to revert back to level one. Small, temporary regressions may occur each school year when a child enters a new grade and a new classroom. The child may worry about her ability to learn the new material, whether new classmates will like her, or whether the new teacher will understand and help her.

Movement up and down this hierarchy of needs will affect a child's behavior and what he needs from the caregiver. If a child changes the way he acts in the childcare setting, the caregiver should check with the parent to see what changes have occurred in the child's life to determine whether some needs are not being met. Even without regression on the hierarchy, each person's lower level needs must be met again and again. One meal doesn't satisfy a person for a day or lifetime and one "well done, nice job" does not make someone feel good for a month.

This hierarchy has great implications for teachers. A child who is hungry, sick, or has no bed to sleep on cannot focus on the tasks we have planned for the day. Basic needs must be taken care of first. Students afraid of violence in their school cannot concentrate on the lecture from the teacher. Lower-level needs must be met before we can become the best teachers we can be.

How does this information help the teacher? When a child doesn't seem interested in the morning activities, she may be hungry, tired, or sick. Determine the cause and then take action to alleviate the problem—provide food, a cot, or nursing care. Only when children's basic physical and emotional needs are met can they learn to like and value themselves. Understanding children's needs is the first step in creating the proper climate for healthy growth and development.

Self-Esteem

The National Association for Self-Esteem defines **self-esteem** as "The experience of being capable of meeting life's challenges and being worthy of happiness" (NASE, 2004). There are two components to self-esteem: competence and worthiness. The worthiness component of self-esteem is linked to human values that provide us with a sense of integrity and satisfaction. A sense of competence refers to believing that you not only have the ability to make appropriate decisions but that you have the conviction to do so.

Because children see parents and teachers as authority figures, they think that the way you treat them is the way they deserve to be treated. In other words, "What you say about me is what I am." When children are treated with respect, they realize that they deserve respect and thus develop self-respect. When children are treated with acceptance, they conclude that they deserve acceptance, and they develop self-acceptance. When they are cared for, they realize they deserve to be loved, and thus develop self-esteem. When they are mistreated or abused, they conclude that they deserve that as well (Parent's Action for Children, 2005).

Children become what we say they are. Teachers and parents are mirrors. What we reflect back to our children becomes the basis for their self-image, which in turn influences all areas of their lives. To put it another way, who our children are is not nearly as important as "who they think they are" (National PTA, 2004).

Our self-concept is based on our experiences. The baby who falls while learning to walk but keeps trying has a healthy self-esteem. The infant is learning that persistence leads to success. For a child to develop positive self-esteem, he needs to feel loved as well as confident in his abilities. If a child is loved but doubts her ability, she will experience low self-esteem. Likewise, the child who feels good about his abilities but is not loved will also experience low self-esteem.

Children with low self-esteem give up easily, are easily frustrated, may be critical of themselves, and are hesitant to try new tasks. Children with low self-esteem often act inappropriately. They may say such things as "I can't do that, I'm stupid." They may knock over another child's block structure because their blocks kept falling over. A child with high self-esteem will just shrug and start again, whereas a child with low self-esteem gives up.

Feelings are built up over a period of years. If, on the whole, day after day and month after month, the child experiences more comfort than discomfort, more balance than imbalance, more attention than lack of attention, he'll grow up with a sense of positive self-esteem and will be more likely to try new things, be a leader, stay away from drugs and alcohol, and do well in school. If, however, all a child experiences is negativity, she will be more likely to abuse drugs and alcohol, skip school, get in trouble with the law, drop out of school, and continue the cycle of low self-esteem. Remember that all children (as well as adults) will experience negative feelings during their lives, but the foundation of those first three years is most important.

We cannot emphasize enough that a child becomes what others say he is. If all the child hears is that he is no good or that he will never amount to anything that is what he will likely become. If a child constantly hears "why can't you be more like your brother?" she will become less like that person. The more we belittle with our words and actions, the less likely the child will grow up with a positive self-worth. But you can make a difference! Don't give up on a child! You may be the only positive figure in the child's daily life (Figure 1-2).

Children with high self-esteem exhibit (Figure 1-3) four common characteristics (Parents Action for Children, 2005):

1. **A sense of belonging:** Children need to feel they belong to a group. This includes family, friends, music groups, sports teams, and so on. Not only do children need to feel special, they need to know that someone will protect and guide them. Children need a sense of who they are and where they came from.

2. **Their uniqueness:** Even though each person is a unique individual, parents tend to focus on similarities rather than recognizing, accepting, and appreciating the differences between themselves and their children. Allow children to excel in activities that they are interested in rather than

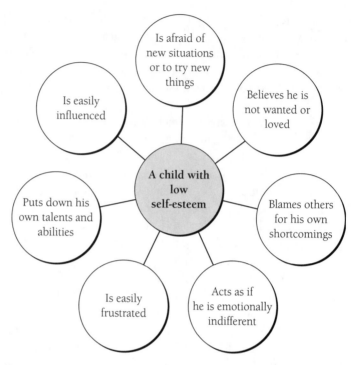

Figure 1-2 Characteristics of Children with Low Self-Esteem

---

1. Acts independently

2. Assumes responsibility

3. Takes pride in their accomplishments

4. Tolerates frustration

5. Handles peer pressure appropriately

6. Attempts new tasks and challenges

7. Handles positive and negative emotions

8. Offers assistance to others

9. Performs well

10. Is flexible

11. Accepts challenges

12. Takes risks

Figure 1-3 Characteristics of Individuals with Positive Self-Esteem

following in their parents' footsteps or living the life that the parents wish they had.

3. **Control over their life:** Children need to feel that they can influence their environment and have some control over their lives. We must teach children the necessary skills to accomplish this. By increasing a child's responsibilities, we are encouraging his or her sense of competence. By allowing children to make decisions for themselves and solve their own problems with our guidance, we help them develop a sense of independence and personal power.

4. **Freedom of expression:** Children must be able to say what they think, openly express their feelings, and ask for what they want and need if they are ever to develop an integrated sense of self. They must be able to think their own thoughts even if they differ from ours. Children need to learn that they may not always get what they ask for, but they should never be blamed for asking.

When children experience a sense of satisfaction in each of these areas, positive self-esteem results. Children need our support and unconditional love; no matter how old they are, even when they make mistakes.

Children need the following for a healthy emotional development:

- **Attachment:** Every infant and child needs the unwavering commitment of at least one adult. This adult is responsive to the infant's needs and thus the infant develops trust. The child needs to be comforted and shown affection as well as compassion. It's not only "cute" when a toddler hugs another child when he falls and cries, but it is also essential for healthy emotional development. A child who is shown compassion will be compassionate toward others.

- **Confidence:** When children feel important, they will develop self-confidence. This self-confidence is increased when adults talk to children. This does not mean "barking orders" but rather communication—a real conversation between adult and child. The adult should show a genuine interest in the discussion so the child realizes she is important. This can be done by showing an interest in children's achievements and encouraging children to take credit for doing something well.

- **Consistency and limits:** Children of all ages need and want boundaries. State reasonable limits based on the child's developmental stage.

The following are some ways you can help build and enhance a child's self-esteem:

- Respect all children.

- Model appropriate behavior.

- Nurture your own self-esteem.

- Value each child as a unique individual with his or her own special interests.

- Think before you speak. Once said, you cannot undo the damage.

- Be honest. Children know when you are not being sincere.

- Actions speak louder than words. Children will do what you do, not what you tell them to do.

- Be positive. Remember the saying "If you can't say anything nice, don't say anything at all." Search for something nice to say to each child.

- Discourage the child's inappropriate behavior, not the child.

- Do not compare one child to another.

- Use nonverbal cues such as a smile, pat on the back, or hug.

- Use positive statements such as "I like the way you. . . ."

- Praise children for jobs well done.

- Encourage children for their efforts.

- Teach children about decision making.

- Allow children "ownership of the problem."

- Offer choices.

- Encourage positive exploration.

- Demonstrate sincere interest in the child's activities.

- Redirect children's negative perceptions.

- Provide positive discipline.

- Be responsible for your own behavior.

- Encourage children to take credit for doing something well.

- Show an interest in the child's achievements.

- Help young children find the words to express their feelings.

- Encourage children who aren't doing well to keep trying.

- Express your unpleasant feelings verbally.

- Accept the child's unpleasant emotions.

- Teach the child how to deal with angry, unhappy feelings.

- Provide ways for the child to feel successful.

- Respond to the child's actions immediately.

- Avoid bringing up the past.

- Teach and demonstrate respect for your own and other cultures and ethnic groups.

- Take photographs of the child.

- Display the child's artwork.

- Help children set realistic goals.

- Help children take pride.

- Let children know it is okay to be silly sometimes.

- Show your sense of humor because it is important for children's well-being.

Figure 1-4 includes a list of words and phrases that can be used to help build children's self-esteem.

AGES AND STAGES

Behavioral Expectations

Very often, adults have unrealistic expectations. A two-year-old cannot be expected to sit still while parents watch a two-hour movie (not very many adults can do that either!). Children go through stages of equilibrium and disequilibrium. During the first

You can say
Good job

        Well done

                Good for you

                            Wow!

Nice work

        That's better

                Correct

                          Good idea
Much better

        What a good idea!

                Bravo
Keep up the good work

        You've got it

                Way to Go

                    I love you (for parents)
I like the way you _____

        I appreciate the way you _____

                I like your _____

You can show
Smile

        Pat on shoulder

                Hug

Figure 1-4 Words and Phrases to Help Build Children's Self-Esteem

few years of life, a child is growing "by leaps and bounds." Often the child's language and social development does not keep pace with his or her physical development. As a result, we are likely to see frustration. Because the child does not yet have the verbal skills to explain that frustration, we will often see biting or hitting. Discipline that works at one stage may not work at another.

For example, a two-and-a-half-year-old is in a stage of disequilibrium and thus may be aggressive one moment and withdrawn the next. Routines are important at this stage. At three years of age, the child is in a state of equilibrium and can handle choices. However, at three and a half, the child is again going through a state of disequilibrium and will have difficulty with change. If we understand these stages and the developmental changes a child is going through, we can help guide children toward self-control and acceptable behavior. Figure 1-5 outlines these stages.

According to research, unrealistic expectations and inaccurate information on child development may raise children who are "overly aggressive," who are more likely to treat situations with intimidation and bullying instead of cooperation. These children may not be able to tolerate frustration, wait their turn, or respect the needs of others (KidsGrowth, 2005).

Behavioral Expectations for Various Stages

AGE 1½

1. Disequilibrium
2. Impulsive
3. Insistent, demanding
4. Wants needs met immediately
5. Easily frustrated
6. Short attention span

AGE 2

1. Equilibrium
2. Confident in motor skills
3. Confident in language skills
4. People oriented
5. Will not share, but is willing to substitute
6. Loving and affectionate

AGE 2½

1. Disequilibrium
2. Inflexible
3. Domineering and demanding
4. Violent and emotional
5. Persistent

AGE 3

1. Good equilibrium
2. Secure with self and others
3. Increased motor skills
4. Increased language skills
5. Makes friends
6. Willing to share
7. Interest have broadened

AGE 3½

1. Disequilibrium
2. Demanding of others, stubborn
3. Hears better when whispered to
4. Stuttering may occur
5. Imaginary companions
6. Feelings are hurt by being ignored
7. Friends are important

AGE 4

1. Equilibrium
2. Talkative
3. Energetic
4. Group play
5. Likes new privileges
6. Figure authority is mom and dad

AGE 4½

1. Disequilibrium
2. Not sensitive to praise
3. Selfish, loud
4. Exaggerates
5. Silly words
6. Name calling
7. Dirty words in public
8. Resists confinement
9. Tries rule breaking

AGE 5

1. Equilibrium
2. Calm, well-adjusted
3. Wants to please
4. Friendly
5. Appreciative

AGE 5½

1. Disequilibrium
2. Emotional
3. Demanding
4. Argumentative
5. Moody

Child's Name _____ Age _____
Observer _____ Date _____

Developmental Checklist (by four years)

Does the child . . .	Yes	No	Sometimes
listen to stories for at least five minutes?	☐	☐	☐
play with other children?	☐	☐	☐
share, take turns (with some assistance)?	☐	☐	☐
engage in dramatic and pretend play?	☐	☐	☐

Figure 1-5 Developmental Checklist by Age

Child's Name _____ Age _____
Observer _____ Date _____

Developmental Checklist (by five years)

Does the child . . .	Yes	No	Sometimes
play and interact with other children; engage in dramatic play that is close to reality?	☐	☐	☐

Child's Name _____ Age _____
Observer _____ Date _____

Developmental Checklist (by six years)

Does the child . . .	Yes	No	Sometimes
engage in cooperative play with other children, involving group decisions, role assignments, rule observance?	☐	☐	☐
■ sit still and listen to an entire short story (five to seven minutes).	☐	☐	☐
■ maintain eye contact when spoken to (unless this is a cultural taboo).	☐	☐	☐
■ play well with other children.	☐	☐	☐

Child's Name _____   Age _____
Observer _____   Date _____

Developmental Checklist (by seven years)

Does the child ...	Yes	No	Sometimes
make friends easily?	☐	☐	☐
show some control of anger, using words instead of physical aggression?	☐	☐	☐
participate in play that requires teamwork and rule observance?	☐	☐	☐
seek adult approval for efforts?	☐	☐	☐

Child's Name _____   Age _____
Observer _____   Date _____

Developmental Checklist (by eight and nine years)

Does the child ...	Yes	No	Sometimes
become less easily frustrated with own performance?	☐	☐	☐
interact and play cooperatively with other children?	☐	☐	☐
participate in some group activities—games, sports, plays?	☐	☐	☐
accept responsibility and complete work independently?	☐	☐	☐
handle stressful situations without becoming overly upset?	☐	☐	☐

Child's Name _____   Age _____
Observer _____   Date _____

Developmental Checklist (by 10 and 11 years)

Does the child ...	Yes	No	Sometimes
handle stressful situations without becoming overly upset or violent?	☐	☐	☐
have one or two "best friends"?	☐	☐	☐
maintain friendships over time?	☐	☐	☐
approach challenges with a reasonable degree of self-confidence?	☐	☐	☐
play cooperatively and follow group instructions?	☐	☐	☐
begin to show an understanding of moral standards: right from wrong, fairness, honesty, good from bad?	☐	☐	☐

Child's Name _____		Age _____		

Observer _____   Date _____

Developmental Checklist (by 12 years)

Does the child ...	Yes	No	Sometimes
enjoy playing organized games and team sports?	☐	☐	☐
respond to anger-invoking situations without resorting to violence or physical aggression?	☐	☐	☐
accept blame for actions on most occasions?	☐	☐	☐
enjoy competition?	☐	☐	☐
accept and carry out responsibility in a dependable manner?	☐	☐	☐

(Some content in this section adapted from Allen, E.A., and Marotz, L., *Developmental Profiles: Pre-Birth through Twelve*, 4E, published by Thomson Delmar Learning.)

SOCIAL AND EMOTIONAL DEVELOPMENT

Understanding the social and emotional development of children is important for determining the appropriate behavior guidance techniques. It is also useful to understand the developmental level of the children's parents as we plan our parent-teacher conferences.

Erik Erickson

Erickson was a leading theorist in the field of lifespan development. He stated that we develop in psychosocial stages and go through developmental changes throughout the lifecycle. There are eight stages or crises we must face (turning point); the more an individual resolves the crisis successfully, the healthier his or her development will be.

Stages in the Life Cycle

1. *Trust vs. Mistrust* (Birth to one year)
   - Infants must feel a sense of trust in their physical comfort, with a minimal amount of fear and apprehension.
   - This trust sets the stage for an expectation that the world will be a good and pleasant place.
   - Attachment is very important; the caregiver's role (mother, father, teacher) is to be certain the infant feels secure and safe.

- When the infant trusts those around him, he will be securely attached and have the confidence to explore his environment. If there is a sense of mistrust, he will be insecure and have little confidence in the world around him.

- The issue of trust arises again at each stage.

- An infant can gain trust later, but can also lose it again during various stages.

- The infant's home environment needs to be safe.

- When we comfort a crying infant, she learns that the world is a good place and we (adults) can be trusted.

2. *Autonomy vs. Shame and Doubt* (Ages one to three)

- Autonomy builds a toddler's mental and motor abilities.

- After gaining the trust of caregivers, infants begin to discover that their behavior is their own.

- They have pride in their accomplishments and want to do everything themselves.

- They are learning to control muscles.

- When the toddlers' needs are met, they become increasingly in control of themselves, generous, and sensitive to others.

- When caregivers are impatient and do everything for toddlers, they may exhibit shame and doubt.

- When adults rush in and are overprotective of the toddler, they reinforce shame and doubt.

- Toddlers need reassurance from adults as well as firmness, loving acceptance, and freedom of self-expression. Failure at this stage brings loss of self-esteem and self-control and may lead to a lifetime of self-doubt or shame.

- Children are not born knowing right from wrong. The parents are tasked with teaching and training them by being fair, fun, and firm; Adults should set limits; too much autonomy is not good.

3. *Initiative vs. Guilt* (Ages three to five)

- Children assume responsibility for their bodies, behavior, toys, and so on.

- Children need a sense of purpose.

- This responsibility increases initiative and a sense of accomplishment.

- Children have a surplus of energy; how they leave this stage depends on parents (and other adults).

- Adults should respond to the child's self-initiated activities.

- The child needs freedom and the opportunity to initiate motor play.

- We should answer children's questions. If motor activity is seen as bad, questions are a nuisance, and play is seen as silly and stupid, a sense of guilt over these activities may persist in later stages.

4. *Industry vs. Inferiority* (Ages 6 to 11)

- "Industry" is a concern with how things are made, how they work, and what they do.

- Children become capable of deductive reasoning.

- Rules become important, especially in competitive activities such as games.

- These are the exploratory years, so children need to try new things.

- Don't push children away. Listen to their concerns (later they won't want to talk to you as parents!).

- Let children see role models who love their work.

- Encourage children's efforts (cooking, sewing, building, etc.) and reward results.

- Don't overdo praise; rather, encourage children's efforts to enhance their sense of industry.

- If you see a child's efforts at making and doing as "mischief or making a mess," the child can develop a sense of inferiority.

- The child's world includes more than home now; school is important.

- The school-age child becomes self-conscious, asking "Am I OK?"

- Rules are important to the child as his value system is developing.

5. *Identity vs. Role Confusion* (Ages 12 to 18)

- Children of this age are searching for ideals; they become critical of parents and society.

- They are looking for a sense of direction.

- Remember anger is a vehicle for breaking away (however, parents need to be mature and try not to shout back at child).
- Sexuality is developing; they are very egocentric (it won't happen to me . . . getting pregnant, death, and so on).
- They are searching for their own personal identity, asking "Who am I?"
- There is confusion about social roles in society as they are going through identity crises.
- If they have a positive outlook of themselves, then they develop a good sense of self-identity.
- Confusion results in negative identity and delinquent behavior.

6. *Intimacy vs. Isolation* (Young Adult)

- Their identity crises have been resolved.
- They develop relationships with friends and coworkers.
- They may "fall in love," which should be a sharing of identities between people freely chosen (you are not trying to change the other person to match that "ideal").
- They have the ability to share and care without losing their own identity.
- There are feelings of isolation when things don't work out.

7. *Generativity vs. Stagnation* (Middle Adult)

- Adults are creating new life and having children.
- There is interest outside of one's self.
- They get joy from their work.
- They will sacrifice for the sake of others.
- They are concerned for future generations.
- If they don't go through this stage with a positive attitude, they become preoccupied with themselves (pamper self).

8. *Integrity vs. Despair* (Senior Years)

- If all other stages are passed through, then they have integrity and pride as well as dignity in life.
- They accept their lives without excessive regrets.
- Adults should come to terms with who they are; if they can't, then despair will result.

- This is a time for reflection and time to enjoy those things they could not do before because of family and money responsibilities.

TEMPERAMENT AND PERSONALITY

Understanding a child's temperament and personality will help you determine what discipline techniques are appropriate for that child. The same behavioral methods cannot be used for all children because no two children are alike. All children are born with behavioral tendencies, however. Thomas, Chess, and Birch (1968) identified nine temperament characteristics as shown in Table 1-1. These traits are present at birth and continue to affect a child's development throughout life. Temperament and life experiences influence a child's personality.

These nine traits combine to form three types of temperaments: easy or flexible, difficult, or slow to warm up. Most children fit one of these three patterns. Forty percent of children are classified as "easy or flexible," 10 percent are classified as "difficult," and

TABLE 1-1 Temperament Characteristics

Temperament	Characteristic	Behavior
Activity level	How active is the child?	Does the child sit quietly or squirm constantly?
Distractibility	How well can the child stay on task?	Can you distract the child by offering a different toy?
Intensity	How does the child react to new situations?	If upset, does the child cry loudly or sit quietly?
Regularity	Are the child's biological functions predictable?	Does the newborn wake every four hours for a bottle?
Sensory threshold	How sensitive is the child to stimuli?	How does the child react to new foods, clothing?
Persistence	What is the length of time the child will stay involved with an activity?	Can the child wait his or her turn?
Adaptability	How well does the child adapt to a new activity?	How does the child respond to transitions?
Mood	How does the child react to the world?	Does the child have a positive or negative outlook on life?
Approach/ withdrawal	How does the child respond to new situations or strangers?	Is the child eager or hesitant when faced with a new situation?

15 percent are classified as "slow to warm up." About 35 percent of children are a combination of these patterns (Kostelnik et al., 2006). By understanding these traits, teachers and parents can use appropriate techniques to fit the needs of the child.

FACTS TO REMEMBER

1. Discipline should not be confused with punishment.

2. Discipline teaches children self-control and teaches right from wrong. Punishment can harm a parent-child or teacher-child relationship by causing a child to distrust.

3. The same discipline techniques may not work on children of different ages.

4. Different ages and stages require different techniques.

5. Children do not behave a certain way all the time. Remember that children are unique and special.

DO NOT FALL INTO THE TRAP . . .

. . . of thinking it is "just a phase." Inappropriate behavior will not just go away and will require adult intervention. Behavioral techniques will be discussed in Chapter 3.

. . . . of being an inappropriate role model. Even two-year-olds will imitate conversations they hear while parents are on the phone. It may not happen immediately; in fact, the conversation (or inappropriate language) will usually occur in church or while visiting your in-laws!

. . . of thinking that what worked once should work all the time. Discipline techniques need to fit the age of the child. Each child is unique and requires different techniques.

. . . of trying to change a child's behavior overnight. You need a plan. Choose only one or two behaviors you want to work on at one time. Have a plan of action and be patient.

. . . of trying to change a child's behavior alone. Include other teachers who work with the child as well as the parents. A team approach that involves consistency is much more likely to be successful.

REFERENCES

Child Development Institute. (n.d.). *Helping our child develop self-esteem*. Retrieved November 20, 2005 from http://www.cdipage.com.

Child Development Institute. (n.d.). *Temperament and your child's personality*. Retrieved November 20, 2005, from http://www.childdevelopmentinfo.com/development/temperament_and_your_child.htm.

Graham, J. (2005). Discipline that Works: The Ages and Stages Approach. University of Maine Cooperative Extension. Retrieved November 20, 2005, from http://www.umext.maine.edu/onlinepubs/htmpubs/ 4140.htm.

KidsGrowth.com. (2005). *What you may (or may not) know about child development*. Retrieved November 20, 2005, from http://www.kidsgrowth.com/resources/articledetail.cfm?id=1176.

Kostelnik, M. J., Whiren, A. P., Soderman, A. K., Stein, & Gregory, K. (2006). *Guiding Children's Social Development: Theory to Practice* (5th ed.). New York: Thomson Delmar Learning.

Lingren, H. G. (1996). *Discipline—An effective life guide*. Retrieved November 20, 2005, from University of Nebraska, Institute of Agriculture and Natural Resources.

NASE. (2004). Self-esteem. Retrieved November 23, 2006 from http://www.self-esteem-nase.org/watisselfesteem.shtml.

National PTA. (2004). Building Self-esteem in your children (Desarrollando la auto-estima en sus niños). Retrieved November 20, 2005 from National PTA http://www.pta.org.

Oliver, K. K. (2002). *Understanding your child's temperament*. Retrieved November 23, 2005, from Ohio State University, Family and Consumer Sciences, http://ohioline.osu.edu/flm02/FS05.html.

Parents Action for Children (2005). *Effective Discipline*. Retrieved November 23, 2005 from http://www.iamyourchild.org/learn/discipline/effectivediscipline/?search=self-esteem

RESOURCES

Web sites for parents

■ Developing your child's self-esteem
http://www.kidshealth.org

- About self-esteem in children
  http://www.cyberparent.com/esteem
  http://www.more-selfesteem.com
  http://www.parentsaction.org
  http://www.iamyourchild.org
- National Association for Self-Esteem
  http://www.selfesteem-nase.org
- Tips for parents to help develop a child's self-esteem
  http://www.cdipage.com
  http://www.schwablearning.org/
- Self Esteem Screening Quiz: Does your child have low self-esteem? Search for the quiz at this site:
  http://pediatrics.about.com

For teachers:

- Rate your self-esteem
  http://www.selfesteem4women.com
  http://www.queendom.com (search under Personality Tests)
- Activities to do with the children: All About Me
  http://www.eduplace.com

WORKSHEET #1

How do you rate? Predict your self-esteem score.

Take one of the quizzes to rate your self-esteem.

What was your score? _____

What does your score mean? _____

List two strengths you realize you have after taking this quiz.

_____

List two weaknesses you realize you have after taking this quiz._____

Name two things about yourself that you could change to make you a better teacher.

_____

WORKSHEET #2

Design a bulletin board and activity that you could do with the children to enhance their self-esteem.

_____
_____
_____
_____
_____

WORKSHEET #3

Here is an activity for elementary children to help enhance self-esteem. How could you modify this activity for preschool children?

> For elementary children: Group eight students together. Fold a piece of paper into eight sections. Put your name on the first fold. Write down one thing you like about yourself. Each student then passes the paper around so that each person in the group writes something they like about everyone in the group.

> Teachers, not students, should select groups.

WORKSHEET #4

Why is it important for you to know and understand Erickson's Eight Stages of the Human Lifecycle? Consider where you are in your life, your family, the children in your classroom, their parents, and so on.

_____
_____
_____
_____
_____
_____
_____
_____

PARENT NEWSLETTER #1

Helping your child develop positive self-esteem

Your child's self esteem can be increased when you

1. tell your child that you appreciate him.

2. tell your child that you love her.

3. spend time with your child.

4. encourage your child to make choices.

5. foster independence in your children.

6. pay attention to what your child is saying.

7. give genuine importance to your child's opinion.

8. take the time to explain the reasons for your decisions.

9. provide positive reinforcement.

10. encourage your child to try new and challenging activities.

11. treat your child with respect.

12. tell your child she is important.

13. tell your child you love him.

14. Let your child know it is okay to make mistakes.

PARENT NEWSLETTER #2

Parenting 101

- Remember, it is not the amount of time you spend with your child but rather what you do with that time.

- The parent is responsible for providing a safe and secure environment for the child.

- Be sure to find a quality child care center if both parents are working outside the home.

- Respond to your baby's crying because it is the only method of communication babies have.

- Have realistic expectations of your child.

- Use age-appropriate methods of discipline.

- Model appropriate behavior for your children.

- Feed your child a healthy diet.

- Read to your child.

- Talk *with* (not to) your child.

2

WHY DO CHILDREN MISBEHAVE?

INTRODUCTION

Children misbehave for many reasons. When a child continuously provokes others or has a behavioral problem, you should look for the cause to get to the "root of the problem." If you can determine the reason for the misbehavior, you may be able to prevent it from happening in the future or at least be better prepared when it does happen. Obviously, you cannot predict or prevent all behavioral issues from occurring in the classroom. However, you can decrease the number of conflicts that occur and have a peaceful day in the classroom. Remember, too, that children from different familial and cultural backgrounds will behave differently based on their upbringing, so what is considered misbehavior in one family might be perfectly acceptable in another. Each child's individual background must be understood before making judgments about behavior.

INAPPROPRIATE EXPECTATIONS

As was discussed in Chapter 1, adults often have unreasonable expectations of children. Children are put into inappropriate situations over which they have no control. For example, you would not expect a 2-year-old to sit still for an entire two-hour movie. A visit to the grocery store at 11:00 PM will likely include the crying of at least one small child who is hungry and tired. How often have you observed teachers (and parents) expecting toddlers to wait 15 minutes for lunch to arrive or expecting 2-year-olds to "sit still and write in their 'journal'"?

The teacher may also have inappropriate expectations with regard to unmet needs, including emotional as well as physical needs as discussed in Chapter 1.

CLASSROOM ENVIRONMENT

One reason children misbehave in the classroom is because of the classroom environment itself. The room arrangement in the classroom can communicate "run, yell, jump" or "walk, use inside voices." Many teachers inadvertently arrange the furniture to encourage running or bumping into other children. The following pages offer some guidelines for arranging your classroom as well as including essential learning centers that should be in every preschool classroom.

Room Arrangement

Our goal as teachers is to provide a supportive emotional and physical environment for our children. When you focus on how a space is organized for children, you can encourage desirable behavior and at the same time prevent or eliminate less desirable behavior.

A classroom can be divided into three key areas: private area, small group learning centers, and large group area.

Private Area

The private area in a classroom is a small semi-enclosed space with room for one or two children. This area is intended to be a place where a child can be alone. It is for the child who feels the need for privacy or realizes he needs to remove himself from a situation. When the child decides to remove herself from a situation and go to the private area, she is learning self-control. No time restrictions should be imposed. The child can return to the group when he or she is feeling better. This area does not have an assigned specific purpose, and it is *not a time out.*

Children need a place to "get away." Remember that children are often in a center for 12 hours a day with someone constantly telling them what to do and where to go. As adults, we allow ourselves to escape, if even for a few minutes, so allow children the same privilege. You may have a loft area, under a loft, or a semi-enclosed area used only for a private area. *Remember that you must be able to see all children at all times.*

Small Group Learning Centers

The small group learning center area is usually designed for four to six children and is used for a specific purpose—art or manipulatives, for example. The teacher may gather a few children for extra help on colors or shapes or do a small group art activity while the rest of the class is involved in center time. A classroom usually has four or five small group centers. Round tables, kidney tables, and rectangular tables can be used.

Large Group Area

The large group area should be large enough for all the children to gather at one time. This area can be used for music and movement or storytelling. The teacher typically brings the materials to this area (flannel board, etc.). This area may also be used for morning "circle time."

Other Factors to Consider

When setting up your classroom, consider these ideas:

- Consider movement and traffic flow. There should be easy access to the various centers in the room.

- Create boundaries for certain areas (blocks, for example). This helps children keep materials in their area as well as preventing others from running into the block structures. It also helps children know where equipment belongs and encourages them to put things away in their proper areas.

- Separate noisy and quiet activities.

- Art, sand, and water should be near a sink.

- There should be enough tables and chairs for all the children. There is usually a round table in housekeeping, another one or two small tables in the art center, as well as two longer tables located somewhere in the room.

- Do not leave a large open area in the middle of the room—children have a tendency to run and not watch where they are going.

Learning Centers

Learning centers are important for the classroom, but which centers should you include? (See Figure 2-1.) At a bare minimum you should have the following:

- Art

- Sand/water

- Housekeeping

- Dramatic play

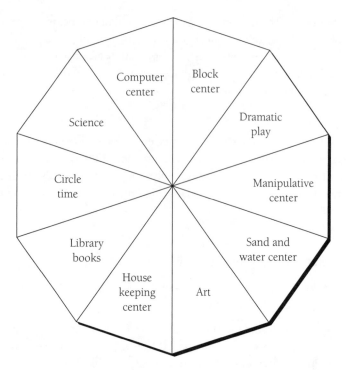

Figure 2-1 The inclusion of multiple learning centers creates a supportive emotional and physical environment that ensures the classroom is organized for the children.

- Blocks
- Library/books (include comfortable seating, such as carpeting, beanbag chairs, and/or child-sized rockers)
- Manipulatives (table toys)—often doubles as the math area
- Science—may rotate and use as special interest area as well
- Music/movement—a large uncluttered area is needed—often the circle area
- Circle time—a large area, usually carpeted

The circle time area is where teachers usually start the day with calendar, good morning, and weather. Additional centers may include computer center, pet center, or woodworking center.

Be sure to develop enough areas so that there are one-third more spaces than the number of children. This allows children a better chance of being able to go to the center of their choice. For example, if there are 21 children, there should be one-third more (7) spaces than children. So there would be 28 slots or choices for children. Children are more likely to get their first or second choice at center time, which makes everyone happier.

Creating a Pleasant Classroom Environment

1. Unclutter your classroom—how many times have you been in a room that was so busy, it seemed chaotic? Get rid of excess materials, or alternate what is in centers and what is stored in cabinets.

2. Modify the lighting—can you turn off the overhead lights and turn on a lamp or two?

3. Lower the ceiling—can you add ceiling tiles to lower the ceiling? It can help absorb sound to make the room not as noisy!

4. Modify the sensory environment:

   a. Create visual interest by adding artwork, plants (make sure they are not poisonous).

   b. Create auditory interest by adding soft pleasant sounds (music, waterfall, etc.).

   c. Create pleasant aromas—scented soap or possibly peppermint to the play dough. (Make sure no one is allergic to anything and children are not in the "everything goes in the mouth" stage.)

   d. Create texture interest—carpets, burlap as a wall hanging, cork bulletin board, fabric wall hanging, and so on.

Classroom Materials

- All materials should be developmentally appropriate—this means both age appropriate and individually appropriate.

- Be sure all necessary materials are available for the project. Children do not wait quietly while you go and ask another teacher for glue.

- Materials should be well organized and stored in the correct location.

- Keep materials visible for children; for example, a bookcase or display is much more likely to attract children's attention than books stacked on the floor.

- Make some materials available and others inaccessible to allow children to be independent and less needy.

- Provide child-sized materials that work well. Remember the old metal scissors that never cut and how frustrated you were? The new plastic with metal edge is actually quite sharp, so be sure children use them correctly.

Allow Children to Personalize Certain Areas of the Room

An easy way to personalize the room is by using the children's artwork. However, don't forget pictures you may take or the pictures children bring from home. Allow children to bring in a special item for naptime. If they have a favorite song, you can play it at naptime. Don't forget a calendar with birthdays and other special days the children may have (Daddy coming home, baby sister born, etc.).

Design Your Classroom

Two catalog companies offer free access on their Web sites to virtual drawing tools, furniture, and materials to help you design your classroom. These sites are listed at the end of this chapter.

Individual Differences

Temperament qualities such as shyness, adaptability, and moodiness can account for many of the differences you see in not only children's behavior, but the teacher's behavior as well.

Learning Style

Have you ever had a classmate who never took any class notes yet would ace every test? Very often we forget to consider an individual's learning style. Just as we all have different personalities, we have different styles of learning. How does learning style relate to guiding children's behavior? The more we understand about how children learn, the better we can organize our classrooms to actively engage all students. If you know what kind of learner the child is, you can develop activities that match that learning style. A child who is immersed in an activity will be too busy to run after Sarah and pull her hair. The key then, is to plan activities throughout the day that appeal to children with different learning styles. For some teachers, this will mean using a different teaching style than they have in the past. One teaching style does not fit all children!

Howard Gardner identified seven ways in which an individual may learn. Characteristics of each learning style are listed here (Reiff, 1996):

- Verbal learners

  enjoy storytelling and creative writing.

  love reading, puzzles, and riddles.

  Teachers and parents should

  - listen and answer the child's questions.

  - read with the child.

  - provide books, writing utensils.

  - visit the library often.

- Logical learners

  enjoy number games, problem solving.

  have strong reasoning skills.

  ask questions in a logical manner.

  prefer order and step-by-step directions.

  Teachers and parents should

  - allow the child to experiment.

  - involve the child in tasks that require organization such as sorting, washing and folding clothes, or organizing their "junk drawer."

- Visual learners

  enjoy designing visual patterns.

  daydream.

  have a talent for art.

  Teachers and parents should

  - provide numerous art materials (paints, chalks, pencils, etc.).

  - visit art museums.

  - allow the child opportunities to solve puzzles.

- Musical learners

  enjoy playing instruments, singing.

  like to listen to environmental and instrumental sounds as well as human voice.

  learn easier if tasks are set to music or to a beat.

  Teachers and parents should

  - encourage the child to sing or clap to the rhythm of music.

  - offer music and/or dance lessons to the child.

  - encourage concerts or musicals.

- Physical learners

  are athletic and active.

  appreciate dancing and role-playing.

  learn by touching and feeling.

  Teachers and parents should

  - involve child in dancing or sports.

  - provide manipulatives.

- Extrovert learners

  are social.

  are leaders.

  enjoy being part of a group.

  work well with others.

  know how others feel.

  Teachers and parents should

  - involve child in group activities.

  - encourage discussion and problem solving.

- Introvert learners

  prefer to work and play alone.

  are self-motivated.

Teachers and parents should

- allow child to work and play alone.

- encourage child to keep a journal.

HOME ENVIRONMENT

Family Crises

At times, you see a subtle or drastic change in a child's behavior. Consider the possibility that there may be a problem at home you are unaware of. There may be a new baby in the house, Dad or Mom may be unemployed or deployed, or there may have been a death in the family. All these situations could cause a child to "act out." Unfortunately, parents are not always willing to share information with you about their personal life. Although they will probably announce the arrival of a new baby, they are less likely to share the fact that a spouse has lost his or her job. The child has probably not been told so the child imagines the worse. You may see the child regress in behavior by sucking his thumb, crawling, and so on. The child may exhibit behaviors that will gain your attention because she is jealous of the new baby.

Family Behavior

There may be drugs, alcohol, or abuse in the child's home. Obviously, the parent is not going to confide in you and disclose this information. When you see a child whose behavior changes drastically with no apparent reason, talk to the child and see if you can determine what is disturbing him. Remember that children imitate the actions of those adults around them. If a two-year-old yells and smacks the doll babies in housekeeping, there is a good chance that this child is being treated like that at home. If you feel the child's life is in jeopardy, take the appropriate steps to ensure the child's safety.

MEDICAL ISSUES

Visual and Auditory Disabilities

"That child just doesn't listen." In some instances, the child may not hear you due to a hearing problem. If you kneel and whisper in the child's ear and she responds, it may be that the child is not ignoring you but rather didn't hear you from across the room. The parents may not have realized that there is a problem. Children who have repeated ear infections also often have speech problems. Because sounds are muffled, so is their speech. After tubes are put in the ear canal, their speech improves dramatically.

If you noticed that Susie is always bumping into things, she may not see the objects until it is too late to change direction. With small children, it is often difficult to determine if there is a visual impairment. Ask the parent if the child sits close to the TV. This could be evident of either a visual or hearing problem.

Allergies

You may see children exhibit uncharacteristic behaviors during certain times of the year or after eating certain foods. The child may have food allergies and become fidgety after eating particular foods. Children who are on medication may be lethargic or overly active when compared to their normal behavior due to certain medications.

Some children may have environmental allergies. The air returns in the building may be damp or dirty causing respiratory problems in children. In extreme cases, this could cause a child to have an asthma attack.

ADD/ADHD

Although preschoolers are normally very energetic, it is possible that you have a child who has ADHD. If the child is on medications, be sure to follow the physician's recommendations.

Tiredness or Discomfort

A child who does not feel well may have difficulty behaving appropriately. Fatigue or anything that causes discomfort can cause children (and adults) to lose control, act aggressively, or defy rules. Being hungry, cold, hot, sick, or hurt are all reasons for children to be cranky and uncooperative. Very young children usually do not even realize that the source of their misery is a waistband that is painfully tight, a sock thread twisted around a toe, or scratchy sand in a wet diaper. Even older children sometimes become negative without recognizing that they just do not feel well.

COGNITIVE DEVELOPMENT

Boredom

A child who is chronologically the same age, but is more advanced academically than the other children may be bored in the classroom. Find meaningful activities for this child or consider placing him half-day in an older classroom. The child should still spend part of his days with same-age peers to provide opportunities for socialization.

Immaturity

Children are typically grouped according to their chronological age. However, children grow at different rates, not just physically, but socially and cognitively as well. A child may not understand the rules. A child who cannot keep up academically with his peers will become frustrated and may act out. Sometimes, it seems that children really want to abide by an adult's request, but somehow they just cannot seem to manage the self-control needed to accomplish what the adult expects.

Often a child who appears bored or immature is actually lacking exposure to learning and stimulation in the home.

CURIOSITY

Children are naturally curious. A child that seems to be "getting into everything" is often actually just being a child.

DISCOURAGEMENT OR FRUSTRATION

Becoming overwhelmed by discouragement can cause a child to feel angry or depressed. When a child reaches a high level of frustration or is frustrated frequently, she eventually loses control. A child who spends all of his hours going to school, participating in extracurricular activities, and doing homework may suffer from stress. A child may exhibit symptoms such as loss of appetite or inappropriate behavior.

DESIRE FOR ATTENTION

If a child feels unwanted or left out, she may not be able to cooperate and follow rules. This issue is discussed in more depth in Chapter 3.

OTHER CONDITIONS

Additional conditions and disabilities may affect children's behavior, including specific learning disabilities, physical and mental impairments, and emotional disorders, such as autism and oppositional defiance. Be sure to thoroughly understand each child's individual personality and upbringing before assuming a "misbehavior" is intentional or even a misbehavior at all.

REFERENCES

Reiff, J. C. (1996). Multiple intelligences: Different ways of learning. Association for Childhood Education International. Retrieved September 30, 2005, from http://www.udel.edu/bateman/acei/multint9.htm.

Stein, H. (2004). Adlerian child guidance principles. Retrieved December 20, 2005, from http://ourworld.compuserve.com/home-pages/hstein/guid.htm.

RESOURCES

Helpful Web Sites
For designing your classroom:
https://www.childcrafteducation.com
http://teacher.scholastic.com. Search under Tools and Class set up.
Other Web sites of interest:
http://venus.uwindsor.ca. Search for information on Dreikur's methods.

WORKSHEET #1

Sketch two floor plans you think would work in your classroom. Use one of the two Web sites listed previously. Be sure to label all areas of the classroom.

3
DISCIPLINE THEORIES
AND GUIDANCE TECHNIQUES

INTRODUCTION

There are many different theories on how to discipline children. As each theory is discussed, you will discover what methods work best for you and the children you care for. You will begin to formulate your own philosophy of discipline. Techniques discussed in one theory often contradict the ideas of another theory. You will also discover that what works best for one child may not work at all for another child.

THEORIES AND TECHNIQUES

Adlerian Theory (Adlerian Child Guidance Principles)

Alfred Adler, a psychotherapist, believed that children should be treated with **mutual respect.** When adults treat children with respect, they learn to respect themselves and others.

Adler also believed that the use of rewards and punishments was outdated. A child would begin to believe that the reward was her right and demand a reward for everything. If punished, the child would believe that gave him the right to punish other children and adults. The child might retaliate in a more severe manner than he was punished by the adult.

In a conflict situation, Adler suggested the following:

- Not talking (but remaining patient and calm) produces a positive outcome. Talking allows the opportunity for the child to become argumentative.

- Withdraw from the situation. If the adult walks away from the child, the child no longer receives attention nor can the child involve the adult in a power struggle.

- Ignore the child during conflict; give attention and recognition when the child behaves well.

- Allow children to resolve their own conflicts. When adults intervene, children do not get a chance to learn how to get along.

Other suggestions by Adler include the following:

- Allow a child to do those things she is capable of by herself. Overprotecting a child does not give the child the opportunity to learn and become responsible for his own behavior.

- Distinguish between positive and negative attention. When a child does not get attention for being good, she will resort to negative behavior that will gain attention.

- Understand the child's goal. Every deed has a purpose. Every child wants to "fit in" or have a place in the group, but not all children have found the acceptable methods to accomplish this. Thus, we see inappropriate behavior.

- Children continue "bad habits" because they gain negative attention.

- Allow the child to be human—we all make mistakes, and no one is perfect.

- Schedule "meetings" and allow the children to discuss those issues that are troubling them. Build consensus. (Stein, 2004)

Adlerian Theory (Dreikur's Behavioral Techniques)

Based on Adler's concept that all behavior has a purpose, Rudolf Dreikur focuses on the four goals of misbehavior. According to Dreikur, there are four "mistaken goals," and children misbehave for one of these reasons:

1. undue attention

2. struggle for power

3. complete inadequacy

4. retaliation and revenge

In his book, *Children: The Challenge* (1964), Dreikur discusses a multitude of discipline techniques to use with children. Although the book was written for parents, most techniques suggested can be used in a classroom setting. You might find it helpful to copy and laminate the list of techniques to post in your classroom:

- Encourage the child—this is the most important aspect of child rearing.

- Separate the deed from the doer.

- Discipline is a continuous process, and its goal is for the child to develop self-respect and a sense of accomplishment.

- Avoid punishment and reward—respect yourself and do not use power to control children.

- Use natural and logical consequences:
  - **Natural consequence** is a direct result of the child's behavior. The discipline technique matches the unwanted behavior; for example, the child who is late for dinner will not eat dinner that night. The child who refuses to put on his hat and gloves when it is cold outside suffers the natural consequence of cold hands and head. Instead of arguing or nagging the child, the child suffers the consequence and thus puts on his or her gloves the next time it is cold.
  - **Logical consequences** are established by parents and teachers and are a direct (or logical) consequence of the misbehavior. A logical consequence takes place when the "punishment fits the crime" as the saying goes. The teenager who misses curfew is not able to go out the next weekend. The child with the messy room cannot go to the movies on Saturday until the room has been cleaned.

- Be firm without dominating. State your case: "We are going to the toy store to buy a birthday present for Tommy's party. I do not have enough money to buy a toy for you," and make that the end of discussion. Don't allow the child to wear you down until you finally give in and buy him a toy.

- Respect the child. All children deserve to be treated with respect. So often, adults are more considerate of strangers than their own children. Treat others as you wish to be treated, including children!

- Induce respect for order and the rights of others. Treat other children's belongings as you want them to treat your belongings.

- Eliminate criticism and minimize mistakes.

- Separate the deed from the doer. Do not expect perfection from children.

- Maintain routine. Children need security and a sense of order in their lives, no matter what their age.

- Take time in training. Children are not born knowing right from wrong; adults need to TRAIN them.

- Win cooperation. Teach the children to get along together to accomplish what's best for all.

- Avoid giving undue attention. Children need attention, but not all the time. Adults are famous for giving attention to the child who is doing what she should not be doing. (When we get to behavioral theory, we will talk about reinforcing negative behavior.)

- Sidestep the struggle for power. You can't force a child, so don't get into a battle. A two-year-old can outlast you!

- Withdraw from the conflict. Dreikur refers to the "bathroom technique," in which Mom shuts the bathroom door to "get away from it all." Obviously, this does not apply in a child care setting.

- Use actions, not words. In other words, do not repeat yourself! The child has now been conditioned not to listen to you: "How many times do I have to tell you to . . .?" Children know how far they can take this. Do you say, "Sandy, this is the last time I am going to tell you" (after about the 10th time)? When you first try using this technique, it will not work because the child knows your past behavior. Remain firm, however, and tell the child you have changed. From now on, you are not going to repeat yourself. Gradually, the child will realize you mean what you say!

- Use care in pleasing; don't be afraid to say no. Parents often want to please their children and may say yes when, instinctively, they want to say no. Remember you are the adult and need to keep the child's best interest in mind. Just because "everyone else can" doesn't mean you should say yes. On the other hand, when you say no, you should give an explanation to an older child (teenagers, especially). This shows it was not an arbitrary decision, but one you gave some thought to.

- Refrain from overprotection. You know the type of children who cannot do anything without Mom (or Dad, or a grandparent, etc.) standing over them: "Be careful, you might fall" or when they do fall, "Oh, you poor baby, come here and let me kiss it and make it better."

- Stimulate independence. Never do for a child what the child can do himself or herself. Why is mom dressing six-year-old Mary every morning? Mary is old enough to dress herself. How often do you hear parents whining about their child not doing anything for themselves, but then the parents don't give the child a chance to become independent? In the classroom, let children wipe the art table when they finish with the play-dough.

- Stay out of fights. When possible, ignore the squabble. Of course, if someone is likely to get hurt, you must intervene. Often, however, when children don't have an audience, the fighting will stop. They are not getting the attention they wanted.

- Mind your own business. Grandma, stay out of it!

- Avoid the pitfalls of pity. You cannot protect your children for life, so you must allow them to make mistakes in order to learn. You need to do this when they are young . . . the consequences can be lifelong mistakes when they become adults.

- Make requests reasonable and sparse so the child is more likely to do what you ask. Some adults are constantly telling children what to do.

- Follow through and be consistent. Do what you say! Don't keep repeating, just do what you say. This means you need to think about what you say before you say it. If you say, "one more word and you will not go on the field trip," then you should not change your mind and bring the child. You may find out you can't leave him behind or start to feel guilty and change your mind. You need to stick to what you say, so think before you speak!

- Put them all in the same boat. For example, "All of you clean up the block area and then we can go outside to play."

- Really listen to what the child is saying.

- Watch your tone of voice; it should be calm, not sarcastic or frightening.

- Downgrade "bad" habits. The more fuss you make over a child's bad habits, the worse they will get.

- Talk *with* them, not *to* them. Think about this and listen to adults. You will hear plenty of commands, but not a lot of "talking."

- Take it easy and have fun together. Life is short, and they will not be young children for long, so enjoy them while you can!

Rogerian Theory

Rogerian theory is based on the premise that children have the capacity for self-direction. As children get older, they are better able to control their own actions. Following are three of the most commonly used strategies:

- Ownership of problem

- Active listening

- I-messages

Very often, adults are the ones who have a problem with the situation and want to change it; that is, they have **ownership of the problem.** However, it may not be a problem to the child, which creates a conflict. When a child owns the problem, we should step back and let him or her try to resolve it. For example: your daughter's bedroom is a mess. You want it cleaned. *Who owns the problem?* You, the adult, because the room is not bothering your daughter. Even though as an adult, you know it needs to be cleaned, it is not an issue with the child. Eventually the child will have to clean her room (can't find clean clothes, homework, etc.).

Active listening stresses listening to children and repeating back what they have said to validate their problems. We listen for feelings ("It sounds like you are very angry" or "My feelings would be hurt if that happened to me, too") but do not solve the child's problem. The goal is to help children learn how to solve their own problems. Negotiation often follows active listening. After a child tells a teacher about a problem and feels that she has been heard, she is more comfortable sharing the issue with a peer. For example, Ava was dressing a doll when Sequana grabbed the half-dressed doll and walked away. Ava expressed her concern to the teacher that she hadn't been able to finish dressing the doll. The teacher suggested to Ava that she tell Sequana how the doll-snatching made her feel. Ava told Sequana that her feelings were hurt when Sequana grabbed the doll before Ava could finish dressing her. Sequana apologized and said she would return the doll to Ava so that Ava could finish dressing the doll. Then Ava could give the doll to Sequana.

Rogerian theory uses **I-messages** to solve problems. These take a lot of practice, and they do not work with all children. There are three parts to an I message:

- When you . . .

- I feel . . .

- because. . . .

For example, "*When you* do not help clean the art table, *I feel* it is unfair *because* I have to clean the table by myself."

Behavioral Theory

Behavioral theory is based on the premise that there must be a strong enough motivator for the child to change his or her behavior or to "do" what the adult wants the child to do. The strongest component of behavioral theory is the use of rewards or other positive reinforcement.

Behavioral theory is used in special education classrooms and is very effective. Behavioral theory is also used in other early childhood settings to a lesser degree; however,it is often used inappropriately. The use of tangible rewards (food, money, stickers, etc.) helps a child learn new behavior or change a behavior, but it does not work on all children. Because our ultimate goal is for a child to be intrinsically motivated, rewards teach children to do the required act to receive the reward. Thus, we often see children who say "what will I get if I do that?"

Rewards do work well as we try to change a child's behavior. Decrease the frequency as you go along and increase the times between the children receiving the reward, and hopefully you will notice one day that the child is doing the behavior without asking for his reward.

One of the most common mistakes teachers and parents make is **reinforcing negative behavior.** For example, you are calling children to pick a flannel piece off the board. Damian is sitting nicely raising his hand (as you requested). Eric is bouncing all over the place and saying "me, me." To get Eric quiet, we call on him next. What did we just teach both boys? Eric learned that it doesn't matter if he sits quiet or not, he will get called first. Damien wonders why he should do what the teacher asked because she ignored his "good behavior." Remember to reinforce positive behavior and ignore negative behavior when at all possible.

The following are a few behavioral techniques:

- **Positive Reinforcement Principle:** Make a big deal over responsible, considerate, appropriate behavior by giving attention, thanks, praise, recognition, hugs, incentives, and special privileges (*not* food).

- **Incompatible Alternative Principle:** Give the child something to do that is incompatible with the inappropriate behavior. "Help me put the napkins on the tables" or "Help me pick out six oranges" (instead of running around the grocery store).

- **Extinction Principle:** Ignore minor misbehavior that is not dangerous, destructive, or embarrassing. (Look the other way.)

- **Satiation Principle:** Allow the behavior to continue (if not dangerous, destructive, or embarrassing) until the child is tired of doing it. The child likes to spit, so have him continue to spit until he wants to stop and never spit again!

- **Successive Approximations Principle:** Do not expect perfection. Acknowledge small steps in the right direction.

Goals of Discipline

The following is a list of the goals of discipline:

- Protect children from harm.

- Teach children right from wrong.
- Teach children to respect the rights of others.
- Teach children self-control.

Negative Discipline

Some adults believe that "discipline" means "punishment." They believe that it is okay to yell, belittle, or slap a child. Negative discipline includes using sarcasm, hurtful teasing, verbal abuse, and humiliation. Unfortunately, these are just a few examples of negative discipline. Negative discipline teaches a child that their world is unpredictable and not safe. It damages a child's self-esteem and self-worth and creates angry children. Taken to the extreme, it is child abuse. Punishment

- lowers the child's self-esteem.
- breeds hostility and anger.
- fails to stop the undesirable behavior.
- leads to child abuse.
- leads to neurotic disorders.
- leads to a desire for revenge and retaliation.
- teaches that might makes right.
- fails to teach appropriate behavior.
- blocks communication.
- gives the child a model for aggression and violence.
- gets misdirected at an innocent party.
- does not promote inner control.
- confuses the child because it is frequently followed by affection, favors, or gifts. This teaches a scary message that love involves hitting and hurting, which is a concept believed by wife beaters and all consenting victims of batterings.
- may cause a child who is usually hit for misbehaving to opt to take a spanking and risk getting caught if his only reason for behaving is to escape punishment.

We need to give children reasons for behaving, not reasons for *not* misbehaving (see Figure 3-1).

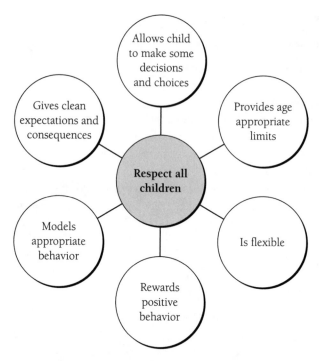

Figure 3-1 Adults who want to give children reasons for behaving use these positive discipline techniques.

TEACHER CHECKLIST

Evaluate yourself and your classroom.

Do you

- _____ treat children with dignity and respect?

- _____ set realistic limits; state message firmly and clearly; be positive?

- _____ change your expectations when you realize they may be unrealistic?

- _____ change the physical environment when necessary?

- _____ ignore some behavior?

- _____ redirect and substitute?

- _____ use consequences as appropriate?

- _____ give a child choices?

- ■ _____ remember to be flexible?

- ■ _____ use nonverbal reminders (a nod, a look with your eyes, etc.)?

- ■ _____ anticipate problems?

Guidance Techniques for Various Age Groups

Guidance techniques to use with infants:

- ■ Know what is reasonable to expect at this stage.
- ■ Make sure the environment is childproof and safe.
- ■ Avoid trouble before it happens.
- ■ Build attachment and bonding so infants develop trust in adults.

Guidance techniques for toddlers and twos:

- ■ Redirect to another activity.
- ■ Substitute one toy for another.
- ■ Ask the child to help you (pick up toys, wipe the table, etc.).
- ■ Physically remove the child from the situation.

Guidance techniques for preschoolers and older:

- ■ Make simple rules and follow through.
- ■ Give children limited choices.
- ■ Use natural and logical consequences.
- ■ Be a role model for the children.
- ■ Act the way you want them to act.

Positive Guidance Techniques

The following is a list of different discipline techniques you can use to help change or modify a child's behavior. This list was compiled using theory, teacher favorites, student suggestions, trial and error, and a few "hand-me-downs." Choose those that you feel comfortable using. Be sure to consider the age of the child and the circumstances of the inappropriate behavior. See Table 3-1 for a list of The Four Mistaken Goals of Misbehavior and Corrective Procedures for the Teacher.

TABLE 3-1 The Four Mistaken Goals of Misbehavior and Corrective Procedures for the Teacher

CHILD'S ACTION AND ATTITUDES	TEACHER'S REACTION	THE 4 MISTAKEN GOALS OF MISBEHAVIOR	CORRECTIVE PROCEDURES
Nuisance Shows off Clowns Is lazy Puts others in his service Keeps teacher busy	**Feels Annoyed** Gives service Is kept busy Reminds often Coaxes Thinks, "He occupies too much of my time."	**Goal 1** ATTENTION "Could it be that you want me to notice you?"	**Never Give Attention When Child Demands It.** Give lots of attention at any other time. Do not show annoyance. Be firm. (Nagging, giving service, advising are attention.)
Stubborn Argues Has temper tantrums Tells lies Is disobedient Does opposite of instructions Does little or no work Says, "If you don't let me do what I want, you don't love me."	**Feels Defeated** Teacher's leadership is threatened. Thinks "She can't do this to me." "Who is running the class, she or I?" "You can't get away with this."	**Goal 2** POWER "Could it be that you want to show me that you can do what you want and no one can stop you?"	**Where Appropriate, Let Child Have Power** Recognize power. Give power in situations where child can use power productively. Avoid power struggle. Extricate from conflict. Don't fight—don't give in. Respect child. Make agreement.
Vicious Steals Is sullen Is defiant Will hurt animals, peers, and adults—kicks, bites, scratches—sore, loser—potential delinquent	**Feels Deeply Hurt** Outraged Dislikes child Retaliates (continual conflicts) Thinks "How mean can he be?"	**Goal 3** REVENGE "Could it be that you want to hurt me and the children in the class?"	**Never Say You are Hurt** Don't behave as though you are. Apply logical consequences. Do the unexpected. Persuade child that he is liked. Use group encouragement. Enlist one buddy.
Feels Hopeless "Stupid" actions Inferiority complex Gives up Rarely participates Says, "Leave me alone. You can't do anything with me."	**Feels Helpless** Throws up hands Thinks, "I don't know what to do with you." "I give up."	**Goal 4** Display of inadequacy "Could it be that you want to be left alone?"	**Encourages When She Makes Mistakes** Make her feel worthwhile. Praise when she tries. Say, "I do not give up with you." Avoid support of inferior feelings. Use a constructive approach.

These are all POSITIVE guidance techniques. Your goal is not to belittle the child but rather help teach self-control. One of the best ways to see a change in behavior is to match the misbehavior with a guidance technique, for example, logical consequences. The most important thing to remember is to treat all children with dignity and respect. When setting limits, be realistic. Be sure to state messages firmly and clearly.

- **When/Then—Abuse It/Lose It Principle:** "When you have finished your homework, then you may watch TV." (No homework, no TV.)

- **Encouragement Principle:** Give encouragement as often as possible. Help the child see the progress he or she has made. ("You got three spelling words correct. That is better than last week!" "Doesn't it feel good to be able to zip your own zipper, make your own bed, and clean up your own spills?")

- **Natural/Logical Consequences Principle:** Teach the child that behavior has consequences. If she forgets her sweater, she gets cold. If he doesn't do his homework, he will get a zero on his homework grade. If the child's allowance is all gone, he or she can't buy the toy in the store.

- **Anticipation Principle:** Think ahead about whether or not the child is capable of handling the situation. If not, don't take the child (field trips, mall visit during holidays, expensive restaurants, movies).

- **Preparation Principle:** Let the child know ahead of time what to expect. ("When you wake up from your nap, you will have a snack and then your Dad will be here to pick you up.")

- **Follow Through/Consistency Principle:** Make a decision, tell the child, and then stick to it.

- **Choice Principle:** Give the child two choices, both of which are acceptable to you. ("Would you rather have red construction paper or blue construction paper?")

- *Be Silly Principle:* Make a game out of it. Have fun. Laugh a lot. ("How would a horse wash his face?")

- **Wait Until Later Principle:** "We'll discuss this after lunch. We both need time to cool off and think."

- **Wants and Feelings Principle:** Allow the child to want what he wants and feel what he feels. Don't try to talk children out of (or feel guilty for) their wants and feelings. This does not mean they will get what they want. Explain the difference between wants and needs: "I need food; I want a new bike."

- **Validation Principle:** Acknowledge (validate) the child's feelings. "I know you feel angry with your teacher and want to stay home from school. I don't blame you. The bus will be here in 45 minutes."

- **Owning Principle:** Decide who owns the problem. If it is bothering you, then you own the problem and need to take responsibility for solving it, *or* you can opt to not let it continue to bother you.

- **I-Message Principle:** Own your own feelings. "When you leave wet towels on the bed, the bed gets wet, and I feel angry. I would like for you to hang them on the hook behind the door."

- **Self-correction Principle:** Give the child a chance to self-correct. Stop talking, preaching, lecturing. Give the child space and time and tell her you will check back later.

- *Redirect Principle:* Pick up the toddler who is about to bite another child, say "no biting," and redirect to another activity.

- **Negative Reinforcement Principle:** Tell the child to take a break or a time out. Give the child a place to go until he is ready to come back and behave appropriately. If the child comes back before pulling himself together, a timer might be necessary. This works well with school-age children.

- **Put It in Writing Principle:** If the child can read, write a note to her, stating your concerns. Ask for an RSVP.

- **Is It Worth It Principle:** Is it really that important? If not, let it go.

- **Modeling Principle:** Model the behaviors you want. Show the child, by example, how to behave.

- **Respect Principle:** Treat the child the same way you do other important people in your life; that is, the way you want the child to treat you and others.

- **Privacy Principle:** *Never* embarrass a child in front of others. *Always* move to a private place to talk when there is a problem (especially in a restaurant, grocery store, classroom, shopping mall).

- **Apology Principle:** When you are wrong, admit it. "I was wrong, I am sorry."

- **Empowerment Principle:** Give children the necessary tools to help them solve their own problems. Let children know that their choices will determine their futures.

- **Positive Closure Principle:** At the end of the day, remind each child that he or she is special. Talk about something good that happened during the day.

- *The Surprise Principle:* React in a surprising way. Start clapping a familiar rhythm ("Twinkle, Twinkle, Little Star") to relieve the tension and get some perspective. It is amazing how, when your head is cleared, you can think better and decide on a more rational way to handle this situation.

- **Use Actions Instead of Words:** Don't say anything. When a child says something inappropriate or hurtful, instead of responding, let the words "hang in the air." Walk away. Take the child's hand and move to another place. Give the child a chance to "hear" what he just said.

- **Take Time for Training Principle:** Often we expect children to read our minds to know how to do things they have never been taught. Although the expectations may be clear to us, children may not have a clue.

- **Human Principle:** Remember, children have feelings too. It is in everyone's best interest to treat children as well or better than we treat other people for whom we are not responsible.

- **The Golden Rule Principle:** Do unto your children what you would have them do unto you! Children will (eventually) treat us the way we treat them.

- **Talk *with* Them, Not *to* Them Principle:** Focus on two-way communication rather than preaching to children. Listen as well as talk.

- **Have Fun Together Principle:** Children love to know that they bring us joy and pleasure. Lighten up and have fun.

- **Help Me Out Principle:** Elicit the child's support. Ask her to help you out (works well with school-age children).

- **Common Sense Principle:** Use your common sense. Does this really make any sense?

- **Change of Environment Principle:** If the children are excited because it's snowing outside, put on your coats and go play in the snow!

- **Chill Out Principle:** It's no big deal! Don't make a mountain out of a molehill. In the grand scheme of things, does this really matter?

- **Hand Gestures Principle:** Develop hand gestures signifying certain words or phrases that only you and the children understand.

- **Pay Attention Principle:** Keep your eyes and mind on what is happening. Don't wait until a child is out of control to step in.

- **Shrug Principle:** Learn to shrug instead of arguing. The shrug means, "I'm sorry, but that's the way it is—end of discussion."

- **Thank-You Principle:** Thank the child for doing the right thing—before he does it.

- **Whisper Principle:** Instead of yelling, screaming, or talking in a loud voice, surprise the child by lowering your voice to a whisper. It also helps you to stay in control and think more clearly.

- **It's Not Personal:** Stay detached emotionally and try to remain objective. Don't take the child's behavior personally.

- **Get On Child's Eye Level Principle:** When talking with the child, get down on the child's eye level and look her in the eye while talking softly.

- **Stay Healthy Principle:** Remember the importance of taking good care of yourself physically and emotionally. Eat well, sleep well, and get plenty of exercise. You will not only be able to cope better, but you will also become a good role model for the children.

- **Cueing Principle:** Give the child a cue, such as a hand gesture, to remind him ahead of time of the behavior you want the child to exhibit. For example, teach the child that, instead of interrupting you when you are talking with someone else, the child should squeeze your hand. This will let you know that the child wants to talk with you (as you return the squeeze), and as soon as you can, you will stop your conversation and find out what he wants.

Topics for Discussion: Praise Versus Encouragement

Although it is important for teachers to help build a child's self-esteem, we must be careful not to place the child on a pedestal. If a child has been told she is a genius, she may decide there is no way she can live up to that expectation. She may be afraid to try new things for fear of failing and disappointing parents and teachers. If we tell a child "Don't worry, it's easy; everyone can do it," the child may believe he is a failure and not as good as others because he could not do the task.

If the child receives too much praise, she might begin to think she is "really all that." Other children won't want to play with the children who always want their way, think they don't have to share, do not help pick up toys, or think they are better than everyone else. Obviously, these children will have social problems as they become older.

We must be realistic with children. Instead of praising the child (good boy, great job), encourage his efforts and actions. This acknowledges the child who is not perfect but is trying to do better. "I can tell you have been working hard on your handwriting" is better than "Wow, great handwriting" when the child scribbled because she didn't care. Be sincere and honest with children.

Encouragement works better than praise for all ages.

Topics for Discussion: Time Out

Time out is used when children have lost self-control. The rule of thumb is one minute of time out for each year of age of the child. Time out can be very effective when used sparingly. Unfortunately, many teachers use this as their first and only method of guiding children's behavior.

Time out is abused when

- used as punishment; for example, a two-year-old is told "You can stay here until you learn how to be nice."

- used as a threat; for example, "Sally, do you want to have to go to time out?"

- it is the only behavior method a teacher knows.

- the teacher doesn't tell children why they have been sent there.

- it becomes a big hole where children disappear because teachers have forgotten about them in the "chair."

Time out should be

- a chance for the child and adult to cool off.

- most effective when the attitude of the adult is kind and firm.

- a place where children go to feel better again.

- available to a child for as little or as much time as he or she decides.

Topics for Discussion: Rewards

Some parents and teachers reward children for everything they do. This can create the child who wants to know "what's in it for me?" The use of rewards does not teach intrinsic motivation; that is, doing something because it makes you feel good or because you know it is the right thing to do.

Rewards can also have the opposite effect on some children. Some children do not like praise or to be noticed. Melissa did not like the teacher telling the class, "Look at Melissa. See how quietly she is doing her work? I want everyone to be like Melissa." Aside from the fact that the other children may begin to resent Melissa, being singled out actually might have the opposite effect than the teacher intended. Melissa might actually start misbehaving so that the teacher doesn't use her as the model child. Melissa was intrinsically motivated. She wanted to do the work for herself, not anyone else.

FACTS TO REMEMBER

1. Each child is unique. A behavioral technique that works with one child may be inappropriate with another child.

2. Do not expect children to be able to do things that they are not old enough to be able to do.

3. Respond promptly to children's needs.

4. Provide a safe, healthy environment for children

5. Patience is needed when dealing with small children.

REFERENCES

Lingren, H. (1996). *Discipline–An effective life guide.* Retrieved November 20, 2005, from http://www.ianrpubs.unl.edu.

Stein, H. (2004). Adlerian child guidance principles. Retrieved December 20, 2005, from http://ourworld.compuserve.com/home-pages/hstein/guid.htm.

RESOURCES

- Discipline, fighting and biting, violent behavior, the depressed child

  http://www.aacap.org (search publications for each of these topics)

- Roots of aggression and nine things to do instead of spanking

  http://www.positiveparenting.com (search newsletters and articles)

- Behavior management

  http://www.ndpass.minot.com

  http://www.disciplinehelp.com

  http://thecol.org

SAMPLE BEHAVIOR TEMPLATE

Location: _____ Time of day: _____

Age of child(ren): _____ Gender of child(ren): _____

Adults involved in the situation:

_____

Conflict observed:

- What actually occurred?
- What did the adult(s) and child(ren) do next?
- What mistaken goal may have caused the child to misbehave?
- What else might have caused this behavior?

- Are there any basic needs not being met (Maslow)?

- Who should have ownership of this problem?

- What could the adult have done? Be specific.

WORKSHEET #1

Use the preceding sample behavior template to help you observe other teachers as well as yourself. By writing down what happened and answering the other questions, it may become clear what went wrong and how you can prevent the scenario from happening again.

WORKSHEET #2

List one scenario where the discipline method you used did not work. List three reasons why you think you were not successful at changing the child's behavior. What could you have done differently?

WORKSHEET #3

Choose one child whose behavior you would like to change. (Only pick one behavior to work on at one time.)

Observe the child for a week, charting his or her behavior, what occurred before and after the behavior occurred, and what action you (or another adult) took that did or did not work. Do you notice any patterns? For example, Johnny always gets cranky around 10:30 AM and starts hitting other children. (Does Johnny get to the center at 6:00 AM? Is he tired by 10:30? Could I allow him to take a short nap in the morning or figure out a way for him to have lunch earlier and then go down for his nap?)

Now decide on a plan of action. List the guidance techniques you think might work and would like to try. Did any of them work? Why or why not?

If none of the techniques work, what do you want to do next? Talk to the parents or director. Make sure you have suggestions ready to offer them when they ask "what do you think we should do?

4

TRANSITIONS

TRANSITIONS

Transition is defined as "a passage from one state, stage, subject, or place to another." In a classroom setting, this time occurs often throughout the day. Transitions occur between home and school, between planned activities, and between routines and special events. Transitions are also often some of the most frustrating parts of a teacher's day. When teachers do not have a specific activity planned for the children, more behavior problems often result because children find ways to entertain themselves. Teachers need to plan activities for these transitions.

During transition, there typically is a change in pace and mood that somehow interrupts the flow of the day. You should be prepared for the "expected" unplanned moments in our day:

- When children are first arriving in the morning

- When children are waiting in line to use the bathroom

- When children are putting coats on to go outside

As teachers, you need to be prepared for the *unexpected* as well:

- Children have washed their hands and are sitting at tables waiting for lunch that is 10 minutes late.

- You are lined up outside waiting for the bus to take you on a field trip.

- A child trips and spills paint on another child.

You need to plan ahead, but be prepared to unplan; in other words, be flexible enough to change or modify what you are doing when you see it is not working.

Have set routines for certain transition times. The children will know what to do and what is expected of them. For example, when children arrive in the morning, they can go to the centers that are opened. When it is time to clean up and go to circle time to begin the day (calendar, morning song, etc.), you could play the same song every day. Children will know that when they hear that song, it is time to clean up and sit down quietly on the carpet.

Transitional Activities

A good transitional activity will set the mood for the next activity as well as help children see the completion of one activity. Transitional activities allow for the children to be involved and reinforce ideas already learned. They can be, in themselves, valuable teaching times. Short familiar songs, finger plays, and body action songs work well for transition times. Planning ahead is the key. Think about any materials you will need.

Save your ideas in a large notebook and add plastic sheets to hold finger puppets or other small items needed for the activity. Remember to keep them simple. A small book bag may also work for you, especially for school-agers or for your field trip days. You can add first aid supplies as well.

Organizing your materials is essential. Some teachers divide their materials into finger plays, short stories, and so on. Other teachers organize by transitions: bathroom time, going outside time, and so on. Decide what will work best for you.

Of all the assignments students must do in my college courses, this is the one they say is the most useful as soon as they set foot in that classroom! Take the time to develop and create your own **transitional notebook.** Following are some samples:

- Have the children pretend to be kangaroos while they are cleaning up. Give each child an apron with pockets so he or she can put items into the pockets until the child reaches that learning center.

- Let the children skip or hop from circle time to their table or from their desk to get their coat. Have each table "move" a different way.

- There may be times when children have to move somewhere as a group, such as down a hall to the cafeteria or to the playground. Sprinkle imaginary "fairy dust" around the children and turn them into a mouse, or other quiet animal. Arm movements could also be used. The children could pretend to be walking on clouds or swimming to the playground.

- For anytime, anywhere transitions, pretend to be a bowl of gelatin and shake all over. Pretend to put on magic ears for listening.

- When it is time to clean up, the children clean to music. When the music stops, the children must freeze until the music starts up again.

Many resource books as well as great teacher Web sites are available to help you find your own transitional activities, including http://www.proteacher.com (search the archive for Transition) and http://www.atozteacherstuff.com (under Tips, choose Sponge and Transition Activities).

5

PARENTS AND TEACHERS

PARENTING STYLES

How adults choose to parent their child affects the way the child behaves in your classroom. What you may consider as inappropriate in the classroom may actually be acceptable in their home environment. For this reason, you must be sensitive as you are talking to the child about his or her unacceptable behavior. For example, a four-year-old who uses inappropriate language in the classroom may be hearing it from his or her parents. Be careful the child doesn't think you are saying his or her parents are "bad." Rather, focus on what is appropriate in the classroom. "In this classroom, we do not use those words. If your parents allow you to use them at home, that is their decision. But it is not allowed in our classroom."

If children are accustomed to a parenting style that conflicts with your guidance techniques, it may be confusing to a young child. That does not mean the child is allowed to behave inappropriately, but rather it may take time and patience on your part to make the child understand that there are different rules for different places. As children get older, they are well aware of this fact.

Parenting styles are often characterized into one of three categories:

- Authoritarian

- Permissive

- Authoritative

Characteristics of the Authoritarian Parent

An authoritarian parent is demanding, strict, uses physical punishment, and does not allow choices. The parent expects obedience and order, and discourages independence. The authoritarian parent also does not like to be questioned.

Authoritarian parents believe that

- children should obey their parents at all times without questioning or talking back.

- children should do as they are told until they are old enough to make their own decisions (and move out of "my" house).

- children should conform to all the parents' decisions without discussion.

- when children do not obey, yelling, threatening, and physical punishment should be used.

Children under authoritarian parents may

- be lacking in curiosity and creativity.

- show limited independence or assertiveness.

- not be able to make decisions, leaving that to others.

- exhibit low self-esteem.

- be aggressive or rebellious

Characteristics of the Permissive Parent

The permissive parent is often seen as uninvolved and spending little time with the child. These parents make few demands, often blaming stress from work as their excuse. Parents set no guidelines and do not assert authority.

Permissive parents believe that

- the children won't listen, so why bother?

- children can get along pretty good if you just leave them alone.

- it is easier to have no rules than to worry about children breaking them.

- their work is stressful and children should understand they are tired.

Children of permissive parents may be

- lacking in self-control.

- exhibiting low self-esteem.

- aggressive.

- easily frustrated.

- immature for their age.

- followers and easily influenced into drugs or delinquent behavior.

Characteristics of the Authoritative Parent

Authoritative parents try to listen and be fair. They encourage independence and offer choices. Parents set standards for behavior, enforce rules, and expect mature behavior.

Authoritative parents believe that

- children should be given choices.

- each child is unique.

- you should listen to what the child has to say.

- it is worth the hard work to allow children to share their feelings regarding family decisions.

Children of authoritative parents are usually

- competent.

- independent.

- responsible.

- able to control their aggression.

- exhibiting high self-esteem.

PARENT CONCERNS

Outlined here are some concerns parents have about leaving their infant or young child in a group setting:

- Lack of supervision
  - not enough staff for the number of infants; not in ratio
  - other demands would shift focus from their child

- worried about their infant being neglected for provider's own children (in a family child care setting)

■ want their child treated as an individual

- want their child's emotional and physical needs to take priority over concerns with schedules and order

■ health

- will my child be ill more in a group setting?

- what do I do when my child is ill?

■ parents want more than custodial care

- play, social interaction

- opportunities for stimulating experiences

- some parents want nothing but "academics"

■ parents want their child to feel loved, secure, and happy each morning when they go to child care

- don't want their infant becoming too attached to provider

■ costs, travel distances, worried about what was really happening during the day

■ parents often anxious about placing infants and toddlers in group care settings because infants cannot communicate yet

- missing the "firsts"

How to Communicate with Parents

You can communicate with parents in many ways, including picture bulletin boards for those parents whose second language is English. Daily sheets are used with infants and toddlers. For preschoolers, you can leave a sheet in the child's cubby; it could just have a picture to let the parent know what type of day the child had.

A monthly newsletter would alert parents to upcoming field trips as well as topics being covered in your thematic units. Parents' night out is also popular. Parents bring a "pot luck" dish to share, and then there is a short workshop on a specific topic by a guest speaker. Children are taken care of at the center during this time. Friday night movies are also another way to involve parents.

Other ways to communicate with parents include the following:

■ Phone a few parents every night until you have called all the children's parents in your classroom. This is a good introduction for the beginning of the year before there are any major conflicts with the child.

■ Use email as more and more families have access to computers and the Internet in their home or at work.

■ Home visits are essential to many at-risk programs such as Head Start.

■ Tape a video of a special project you did with the children. Parents take turns viewing the tape at home with their children. Make sure all the parents are okay with this before you proceed.

■ Ask parents to bring pictures from home for the children to share with the class.

■ Help children make an "All About Me" book at the end of the year. Add some of the children's artwork, pictures you have taken of the children over the year, as well as any dictated stories the children may have done.

STRESS

Working with children can be both physically and emotionally demanding so teachers must keep themselves healthy. Following are some activities that will help reduce stress. Although these activities are intended for the teachers, several can be used with the children as well. Some form of exercise should be included in your daily schedule. This does not mean that you must walk 3 miles a day or put in 30 minutes at the gym. There are opportunities to exercise during your daily routines.

Breathing Exercises

Deep breathing is an easy stress reliever that has numerous benefits for the body, including oxygenating the blood, which wakes up the brain, and relaxing muscles. Breathing exercises are especially helpful because you can do them anywhere, and they work quickly so you can destress quickly. Breathing can help you become more physically relaxed and mentally centered. Follow these breathing exercise steps:

1. Sit in a comfortable position.

2. Close your eyes, but keep your head up and your eyes (behind your lids) focused on the horizon.

3. Take one deep, cleansing breath, and hold it in for the count of 6. Then breathe normally and focus your attention on your breathing. As you breathe, inhale through your nose and exhale through your mouth.

4. If your thoughts drift toward the stresses of the day ahead or of the day behind you, gently refocus on your breathing. Feel the air move in, and feel the air move out.

5. Continue this for a few minutes, and you should notice that your body is more relaxed and your mind is calmer. Enjoy the rest of your day!

Exercises

Be sure to check with your doctor before beginning any exercise program; then consider these exercises:

- Strengthen your back.

    1. Practice good posture. Stand tall. Shoulders should be back, arms at your side. Breathe deeply and exhale slowly.

    2. Do a "Good morning" stretch (stretch arms to the sky, then bend and reach to the ground).

    3. Hug yourself. Each day, try to reach your arms further around your back.

- Neck and shoulders

    1. Lower your chin to your chest and hold for at least 10 seconds. Slowly roll your head to your left shoulder; hold for 10 seconds and then pull your shoulder up to meet your head. Repeat with your right shoulder.

    2. Shrug your shoulders for 15 seconds.

- Arms and hands

    1. Place your hands over each other behind your head. Bring your elbows forward as far as is comfortable.

    2. Place your hands together behind your waist. Pull your hands away from your body as far as is comfortable. Repeat three times.

- Legs and hips

    1. Stand with feet together for 10 seconds; then stand on tiptoe. Hold for a few seconds; repeat 5 times.

2. Put your hands on your hips; put one foot forward and bend both knees slightly. Stand straight again, place your heel on the ground and point your toes up to stretch your leg. Repeat with the other foot.

RESOURCES

Helping children cope with stress

- http://www.ces.ncsu.edu

- http://stress.about.com

WORKSHEET #1

Name at least five other ways you can think of to communicate with parents. Don't forget that some of your parents may not be able to read or may use English as their second language.

ADDITIONAL WEB SITES FOR TEACHERS AND PARENTS

- **http://www.parenting.org:** The group of professionals who represent Girls and Boys Town National Resources and Training Center created this Web site to offer practical parenting advice on a range of topics. Girls and Boys Town has provided amazing services to boys and girls for decades.

- **http://parenting.ivillage.com:** This Web site has helpful information and advice for parents dealing with children at all developmental stages. The topic areas begin with "Trying to Conceive" and progress through the teen years. They offer ideas on crafts, consumer information, and helping Mom pamper herself more. They offer advice and information on an extensive list of topics.

- **http://www.positiveparenting.com:** "Positive Parenting is dedicated to providing resources and information to help make parenting more rewarding, effective and fun!" This Web site, created by well-educated professionals, offers audio files for parents to listen to on certain topics as well as mp3 files, which parents can download and listen to at their leisure. The Web site also offers classes.

- **http://parenting.aol.com:** This Web site is an extension of *Parenting Magazine*. The articles and topics are extensive and comprehensive, and you can search by the age of the child(ren) you are working with. They also offer a homework/learning helpline.

■ **http://parenthood.com:** This Web site highlights adoption, family finances, special needs children, and grandparenting.

■ **http://www.americanbaby.com:** *American Baby* magazine Web site concentrates on conception and pregnancy, and contains volumes of information on newborns through age two. The Web site also offers a newsletter with free membership.

■ **http://www.fathermag.com:** This Web site for fathers offers information on "Fathering on the Fringe," "The Joy of Fathering," "The Importance of Fathers," "Custody and Divorce," "Second Wives and Second Families," "Fathers and Sons," "Fathers and Daughters," "Single Fathers," and more.

■ **http://www.tnpc.com:** This Web site is produced through The National Parenting Center, which was founded in July of 1989. Their mission statement states that they began this Web site "with the intention of providing the most comprehensive and responsible parenting advice to parents everywhere. The advice provided is furnished by some of the world's most respected authorities in the field of child rearing and development." The Web site offers a unique teen and child personality quiz that attempts to help you understand your child better.

■ **http://www.familyeducation.com:** This site deals exclusively with education concerns that a family might be faced with. The site gives parents advice from Dr. Seuss, guides parents through choosing the right school, helps parents with handling parent-teacher conferences, offers homework help, and provides information on applying to college. The resources are categorized by age and interest.

■ **http://childparenting.about.com:** This Web site offers a broad selection of information covering discipline, health issues, development, family issues, and so on, as well as a great deal of academic support with homework helplines, advice on computers, helping children succeed in school, and effective study tips. The site also guides parents in selecting toys, gifts, and other family consumer needs.

- **http://www.kidshealth.org:** KidsHealth provides doctor-approved health information about children through adolescence. KidsHealth has separate areas for kids, teens, and parents and includes tons of features, articles, animations, games, and resources. All the information is created and developed by experts in children and teen health.

- **http://www.ed.gov:** This site offers various links to help your child academically (for example, "Helping Your Child Learn History or Science"). Search for "parents."

- **http://www.internet4classroom.com:** This site offers information for parents to help their children. Links include reading, discipline, family, and schoolwork.

- **http://www.futureofchildren.org:** This site offers different journals you can read about issues children are facing such as obesity, social mobility, and so on.

- **http://www.magickeys.com:** This site offers free stories you can read to your children and has books such as phonics, home schooling, children's books, and puzzles.

- **http://www.sesameworkshop.org:** Sesame Street games and short stories about Sesame Street characters facing certain fears and issues such as fire safety, immunizations, first day of school, and so on are the highlights of this Web site.

- **http://www.childrensmusic.org:** This site offers resources for parents to monitor their children's music. It has age-appropriate music for children and gives a comprehensive list of children's recording artists.

- **http://www.storyplace.org:** This site is a digital library for children offered in English and Spanish with links for selecting age-appropriate activities and stories.

- **http://www.chkd.org:** This site has information for parents on positive discipline and how to reduce stress with newborns and small children. It also gives information on health and other issues such as CPR.

- **http://www.stophitting.com:** This site gives information on how to stop spanking and offers alternative ways for disciplining.

- **http://www.positivediscipline.com:** On this site, supported by Oprah, you can get information on positive discipline and ask questions and get a doctor's response.

- **http://www.foreverfamilies.net:** Guiding children, family challenges, and issues facing families are topics that can be addressed on this site. It covers behavioral problems, keeping tabs on teens, and strengthening relationships.

- **http://aappolicy.aappublications.org:** This site gives developmental approaches to discipline, strategies for effective discipline, and recommendations on how to change behavior.

- **http://www.nncc.org:** This site promotes positive behavior and gives you links to help children who have multiple problems such as abuse.

- **http://www.practicalparent.org.uk:** This support site for parents and teachers includes a discussion board where you can ask questions and get answers on child behavior, and parenting tips such as stress and how it affects your child and their behavior.

- **http://www.parentingweb.com:** This site discusses discipline verses punishment, and helps steer parents and teachers to guide children to responsible behavior.